On the Brink

Poetry and Politics

Estella Lauter

Sturgeon Bay, Wisconsin

Four
Windows
Press

Four Windows Press
231 N Hudson Ave
Sturgeon Bay, Wisconsin 54235
www.fourwindowspress.com

Publisher's Note: This is a work of poetry. Names, characters, places, and incidents are a product of the author's imagination. Locales and public names are sometimes used for atmospheric purposes. Any resemblance to actual people, living or dead, or to businesses, companies, events, institutions, or locales is completely coincidental.

Book Layout © 2024 BookDesignTemplates.com

On the Brink by Estella Lauter -- 1st ed.
ISBN 979-8-9905946-3-0

Praise for *On the Brink*

Publisher's note: This book is an extraordinary book. Estella Lauter is both a scholar and a poet, having produced significant books in both modes of writing. Door County, Wisconsin, where she is from, has many accomplished poets, among whom she is now an Elder, as its third Poet Laureate, a founder of the critique group, Belles Lettres, the Door County Poets Collective, and, with her husband, Chuck, of the Dickinson Poetry Series. As Max Garland says,

Estella Lauter's collection *On the Brink* makes its political and cultural concerns clear from the beginning. In poem after poem Lauter passionately makes the case that poetry, if genuinely concerned with *life*, is also necessarily concerned with *political life*. Utilizing personal history, wide historical knowledge, and deep regard for the wisdom inherent in both language and the natural world, these poems do not shy away from overt political or cultural stances, nor do they fail to recognize what's at stake when our loudest and least empathetic public voices seek to separate rather than connect us.

The poems here are empowered by specificity, close observation, and deep respect for the natural world. "The Earth remains, not quite intact/ but quivering with light we could still share," reads a poem near the end of the book; increasingly in these latter poems, *On the Brink* suggests that what hope we have as a people, or species, may depend upon our attention to the lessons and language of the natural world (the living systems of Earth) as well as an increasing awareness of what connects us. Lauter also reminds us of poetry's ongoing role in nurturing that awareness.

Max Garland is author of "The Postal Confessions," the Juniper Prize for Poetry in 1995; "Hunger Wide as Heaven," the CSU Poetry Center Open Competition in 2006; and "The Word We Used for It," the Brittingham Poetry Prize in 2017.

Previous Books by Estella Lauter

Pressing a Life Together By Hand. Georgetown, KY, Finishing Line Press, 2007. New Women's Voices Series, No. 53.

The Essential Rudder: North Channel Poems. Georgetown, KY, Finishing Line Press, 2008.

Transfiguration: Re-imagining Remedios Varo. Georgetown, KY, Finishing Line Press, 2013.

You Never Said. We Didn't Ask: A Legacy from World War I. Georgetown, KY, Finishing Line Press, 2018.

Women As Mythmakers: Poetry and Visual Art by Twentieth Century Women. Bloomington, IN: Indiana University Press, 1984.

Estella Lauter and Carol Rupprecht, *Feminist Archetypal Theory: Interdisciplinary Re-Visions of Jungian Thought (with an Introduction and a Theoretical Conclusion).* Knoxville, TN: University of Tennessee Press, 1985.

Joseph Gibaldi, Jean Pierre Barricelli and Estella Lauter, eds., *Teaching Literature and Other Arts.* NY: Modern Language Association Press, 1990.

Cover Photo by Kristin Lauter

Cover Design by Ethel Mortenson Davis

Author Photo by Chuck Lauter

Dedication

For all the members of the writing groups who have given my words the space, time and careful attention to develop as poems and have encouraged me always to go further. I especially remember my writing group in Appleton with Ellen Kort, Rusty McKenzie and Laurel Mills; in Door County, the Wallace Group, Word Women and Belles Lettres; at Bjorklunden, seminars with Marilyn Taylor and Robin Chapman; and on the internet, The Grind. Thank you all for keeping the faith in poetry.

Forward: A Note on "Poetry and Politics"

Wherever two or more people live together, and the need for some kind of "government" arises, politics will also be present. It may be subtle and gentle, as it was in the actions performed by my grandmothers when they saved the lives of my mother and father, or cruel and destructive as in war zones, but it is likely to come into play whenever people disagree about "how to live," or "what to do." Politics is everywhere around us—more so all the time with the addition of social media to our systems of communication. Even the most private event (say, a miscarriage) may become political in this environment. Perhaps it has always been so. This book reflects the many ways poetry may interact with politics. It can awaken a reader to the presence of politics, witness a condition caused by politics, offer another way of seeing a political conflict, call out or satirize a political act, participate in or reframe a political argument, write back to those in power, exhort a reader to act, see beyond the present and imagine a different future. Poetry can seek to *intervene* in politics in many ways. There is no necessary division between poetry and politics. Poetry is not obliged to be silent about political realities.

In the United States, we have not yet produced a Pablo Neruda or Vaclav Havel, who wrote poetry and led a nation, but plenty of poets here and abroad address the issues of our time. Whether or not we can be effective in moving a larger polity remains to be seen.

Contents

Conundrums..31

Epigraph:
Peter Piper

As we have known since childhood,
he must have been a politic
judicious man who took advantage
of the season, a citizen in a civil
place that celebrated his right
to harvest more peppers than
one man would need to feed himself.

Perhaps his town did not set limits
on the number of pecks he could pick,
but it probably had a policy to keep
its market safe from plundering.

In his time, whenever that was,
there may have been a council that
decided what to do if his neighbors
protested his habit of pickling peppers
before they were picked.

It's complicated.
We cannot just reject everything political
as scheming, cunning, lowdown nonsense.

Peter's polity must have protected
his pickles from politics,

which makes the world go around,
often faster than we can say
Peter Piper picked a peck . . .

I

It all began with women

Incubator

Anna Hooker Lawrence, 1880-1938

Her third daughter, premature, was born
at seven months, three pounds, with hernias
in her belly wall, intestines bursting through.

The doctor said *Now Anna, don't you fret,*
you can have more. But she called her sister Naomi
from upstairs and asked her for clean cloth
to bandage up the baby's gaping wounds.

While the untimely child hung on, she sewed
buttons on cardboard, lined them with cotton, cut
strips from old sheets to hold the organs in.
Then, lifting the baby between her elbow and palm,
she nestled her broken treasure in a box for boots
and kept her on the oven door of the old wood stove.

All that hot summer and a year, she changed
the dressings, nursed the fragile body, sang,
canned, churned and cared for children late
ever so late into the night with her sister.

In other times, she might have been feared
for witchcraft. The numbers prime: her third
girl, born in the seventh month of nineteen-
o-seven. But she knew neither medicine
nor magic, only the steady, ragged rhythms
of pressing a life together by hand.

That Craggy Line

Estella Clark Loomis, 1882-1920

Even in a snapshot on the short front lawn
with Grandpa cuddled against her side, she looks
impressive, this stately woman I never met
who taught school before three boys were born.
The doctor warned the third should be her last.

She sent her sons to study violin
with hot stones and heavy wool blankets
to warm them in their single horse-drawn sleigh.
But I will never know how hard she worked
or what she felt. Everyone said that she
was wise, but no record of her words survives.
Only a muslin friendship quilt, now brown
and stained, still bears her signature in red.

One day, the family story goes, my father,
a child of six, was laid in the parlor to die,
his forehead split by a horse's hoof, his brain
exposed. She offered strands of her long hair
to bind the wound the doctor claimed would never
heal, and, sure enough, those stitches held
though she herself soon died in childbirth.

Between us now, besides the photo, the quilt,
our common name, is just that craggy line.

A Poet Asks Why I Write Political Poems

Because of the zigzag scar that ran
down my father's forehead
where his favorite horse
kicking up her heels
had opened the skin
and exposed his skull.

In order to accept
what his doctor later called
his *eccentricities,* among them
a new job every year or two
up and down the Coast
new challenges to prove
his brain was not damaged
by the accident.

Because my mother and I
could only observe, never change
what had happened or his response to it

I learned early
to notice the pain of others.

Shadow Woman

You ask what shadow lies beneath the gentle manner
of my daily life. It's anger, born of my father's grief
at the loss of his mother in childbirth
for which he blamed his father
and, inexplicably, my mother,
who never lived up to his image
of female perfection.

There I was between them
watching him tear her down
needing to keep them together
but also feeling it was not good
to be a woman.

I caught his anger like the flu
and turned it against him, although
my mother had schooled me
by example in mercy.

And I passed a torch for justice to my daughter
before I understood its shadow power.

The anger doesn't fade away
but now when it comes, I talk with it
find ways to use its force for women.

On Being Diminished

He was a good man
didn't hit her
but he hurt her
all the same

just ignored her
or implored her
to do his bidding
without complaint

If she sat down
after working
he'd berate her
interrogate her

till she was ready
to disappear
Or when her voice rose
up against him

he'd reject her
as inferior
leave the room
go on the road

feeling proud that
he hadn't hit her
though he hurt her
pared her down.

Is That All There Is?

As sung by Peggy Lee

A sad song, a stoic song
one I loved without knowing why
because in the year it won a Grammy
for Peggy I moved west
joined a new community
had a child and life suddenly
moved so fast it felt like
a fire, a circus, love, death
all at once
no time for disappointment

But before that flurry
were years of waiting
for parents to come home from work
the next move north or south
friends who lasted more than one year
anything to show I had been on earth
even a tombstone preferable
to leaving no trace at all

And now I think
those lean years made
the others seem like
more than enough
too much of a good thing
more than I needed
for one life

So, if I could sing like Peggy
ever so slightly off key
in that throaty voice

I'd ask why I had so much
and others so little
Why can't everyone be dancing?

Confession

There was a time when I rarely left
my house without an amulet

The Māori lizard from a poet-friend
in my pocket
a Zuni butterfly ring on my finger
the gemstone my daughter gave me
last birthday on a chain
around my neck
a Hogwarts mug on my desk
Zapotecan warrior on the windowsill
Dream-catchers everywhere

No crosses or medals but otherwise
I was an equal opportunity employer

I even burned some sage one time
before a meeting when I was to be
the sole woman in the room

I'll never know exactly what they warded off
but here's the proof they worked

I survived mostly intact
in a man's world

Dear Saint Joan

To Jeanne d'Arc, 2004

I've been meaning to write you
since reading Shaw's play
and seeing Cindy Sheehan camped
at the edge of Bush's sprawling ranch
in Texas to protest the war that killed her son.

From your lofty view
with the wisdom of centuries behind us,
do you ever reconsider the path you chose?
All that courage lavished on a king
only to be burned for your beliefs.

Are you still quite certain it was
God who directed you to fight?
Didn't all the kings
who pushed the Cross eastward
cloak their desire for power
as the will to save?

So, what do you think
of Cindy's stand on the border
refusing the lure of violence,
calling on others to join her plea
to think of the children.
If we betray them
who will tend the world?

You were scarcely more than a child
yourself when you put on the armor
that earned your place in history.

Do you never wish that someone
in the Dauphin's court had said
think of the children?

Maya Angelou
at the Union Theater, 1990

She gave a long, rambling talk that night
no notes, just memories, encounters, optics
on experience in that mesmerizing voice
from deep within her tall, straight form,
but that is not what I remember most.

After the program we went backstage
where maybe sixty people, mostly young,
milled around waiting to give her a hand,
quietly pay our respects, not more.
So, when she swept into the room

and we felt her electric energy fill the air,
we gasped, taking it in along with her words.
Press the brain, she said. Then in her sixties,
she had begun to study Japanese, she said,
her seventh language. If she could do that,

then think what younger folk could do.
If she, with little formal education, could serve
on famous Boards, what could members
of a great university do if only we would
press the brain harder, work it out

like a muscle that has not reached its
full size. And then she went from student
to student in the crowd, putting her hands
on both sides of their heads, and pressing hard,
saying over and over, *press the brain*.

One of the women in my class
received this laying on of hands.

It was a call she needed, as did I.
Although I didn't feel those hands
her words press on.

Celestial Pablum

Papilla Estelar, 1958,
  a painting by Remedios Varo

Have you ever seen such a humble figure of power?
A tall woman seated in a slight gazebo feeding
no less a *personaje* than the moon itself,
but a waning moon, upon which the earth
still depends for tides and who knows what else
given the way all things eventually connect?

She is not the one her culture would have chosen
but men were busy making war and money.
She wears a long brown sheath and grinds
the food from starlight patiently to keep
her charge alive, though caged, and safe
from greedy explorers who would surely
plunder it if they could. Ever calm,
she will never leave this old man alone.

II

Belief/Poetry

Belief

Everyone has to believe in something, and I believe in Poetry. It happened in a high school course on the New Testament. *In the beginning was the Word.* Now there's the Truth, raw as a salmon swimming upstream. I often fear the salmon won't get there. Poetry requires so much good will--attending to the voice of a stranger on a page. I continue to believe in Poetry, *the word made flesh*, precisely because it always lies there waiting at the beginning to shape what we see and don't. Because it still leaps out of the water of syllables into fresh air to change our course. Because without it, I cannot imagine a good life in my country, where many seem to believe only what they are told from media pulpits by corporations now enshrined by law as human, more powerful than you yourself in front of your morning mirror.

> Some days, Venus swims
> straight to her half-shell,
> to rise in naked glory.

Truth, Beauty and the Deer

There's a deer outside my window, munching
on weeds along the escarpment, her ears flicking
every few seconds as she hears sounds that might
mean trouble, requiring her to dash further
into the forest. Soon she decides to lie down.

Unusual for her kind,
which usually travels in pairs or families
(we say, *if you see one, watch for another*)
she's on her own, just resting and chewing
but otherwise so still I would not see her
if I did not know she is there.

We say that beauty is in the eye
of the beholder, recognizing different
standards, personal and cultural
but is there anyone alive
who would not find her beautiful?

Now she rises, hearing my husband's
booming voice, and when I look again
she's gone. She can't be sure
of his intent, can't wait to see
if he has a gun. She knows,
whether from experience
or collective knowledge
a kind of intuition
that truth is hard to find.

The Poems of Our Climate

. . . one would want more, one would need more,
More than a world of white and snowy scents.

Wallace Stevens, *The Poems of Our Climate*, 1938

Between the great wars of your century,
Stevens, old master, you said the image alone
is not enough to make a poem. The cold
bowl of pink and white carnations

cannot suffice even if it makes our *torments*
easier to bear. The one who sees must be there
in the poem, the *vital I*, no matter how imperfect,
among the *flawed words and stubborn sounds*.

You could not have foreseen how that *I* would
blossom once the wars receded to far-away lands,
how soon all its torments would be personal
as poets confessed their own imperfections.

But you knew that poetry must change
to meet the new needs of each age,
no other era exactly the same, no matter
how many turns the wheel of fortune takes.

Now here we are, needing *truth* from poems,
because it is missing in action, gunned down
by illusions more clever than the eye can see:
political spectacles more fantastic than fiction.

If the poems of our climate can't be completely
true, let them at least *try* for close-ups
of a world we recognize as real, even if
only in shards, beneath these powerful lies.

What Poets Can Do

Can we say anything about a war
like the one we face in Gaza?

What if we honor our love of words
by pointing out when a powerful man
misuses them? Take, for example
the mantra that Israel's war is noble:
Civilization against *Barbarians*.

Barbarians: a word no longer used
elsewhere for those who have lived
continuously on land desired by others.
Beasts insults a whole kingdom of animals
who get along without rockets and bombs.
Mothers, pregnant women, infants, children
half the population are not *brutes*.
People in Gaza are not *savage* by nature.
They, too, are Semites, long-ago neighbors
in Judah—some recognized there as friends.

Words define what we see or don't.
Civilization: often a cover for covetous desire.

Personification (after Layli Longsoldier)

Personify—v. tr. represent (an abstraction or thing) as human. Oxford American Dictionary

Didn't it strike you as odd when the U.S. Supreme Court decided that Corporations were people with free speech who could fund candidates in democratic elections?

A Corporation is designated as an organization on paper by a legal office.

Weren't the Justices engaging in personification?

We all do it—as when a computer or a car stalls, and we ascribe intention to it.

Personification has been a staple of poetry ever since Homer recited *The Iliad*, where natural phenomena appear as gods and goddesses in human form with human emotions.

Did the Supreme Court write poetry in *Citizens United*?

What about the Alabama Supreme Court's decision that human life begins at conception, so a fertilized egg is always already a human being?

But many eggs may be fertilized without being implanted; are they all human with, say, rights to health care and burial or cremation?

How would Alabama gather miscarried eggs?

Would already-living-human-beings suffer because of astronomical costs for reproduction?

What does it mean to be human if such rudimentary life is counted?

Is this not personification at its most fantastic?

Now that courts are writing poetry, perhaps poets should write laws.

To a Future Archeologist

Remembering that Modernist American poets
were later accused of being apolitical
I insist that the absence of a certain figure
from our poems (he-who-shall-not-be-named
except as *T.*) should not be understood
as a failure of concern for the nation.
Since the media are obsessed with every lie
he utters, it is our task to turn attention
elsewhere—to children who need food,
shelter, books, broadband, facts
that can be verified; parents who need
child-care, health-care, elder-care;
immigrants who need security;
migrants who need relief from violence
none of this on offer in the garish
towers you dig up across our land.

Attention! There is more truth
in a single poem than in the hundreds
of gold toilet seats you will recover.

Peace, Peaceable, Peaceful, Peacemaker

Amity
Brotherhood
Concord
Détente
Easygoing
Friendliness
Goodwill
Harmony
Irenic
Just
Kind
Lamblike
Mediator
Nonviolent
Objector
Pacific
Quiet
Relaxed
Serenity
Tranquility
Untroubled
Variation accepted
War in masquerade
X for the Great Unknown
Yin/yang
Zed for the end of strife

With such a long history in words
(from Chinese, French, German, Greek, Latin)
wouldn't you think we could hold on to Peace
for more than a few hours at a time?

Turmeric and Cumin

I've used these spices for decades
but now, alone together, they mean
Morocco, its signature *tagine*,
with a little meat and an array
of vegetables or beans
cooked slowly over coals
for hours, their flavors changing
the taste of carrots and onions
penetrating the lamb or chicken
and leaving an unmistakable aroma
in the air that isn't semi-sweet like cumin
or sharp and clean like turmeric,
a pungent smell that fills our house
and brings back memories
of desert people, Berbers,
who live hard lives
growing and making almost
everything they use,
often walking miles for water,
understanding *freedom*
by paying its full price.

Kind, A Brief History

Kind, from the Old English *gekynd*
meaning nature at first, then class.
In the time we now call the Dark Ages
if something was *gekynd*, it was
a Law of Nature, an expectation
people could count on. Later,
it meant things similar enough
to each other to bring together.
Later still, wordsmiths added kindness,
meaning a gentling bond among kinds.
But the dictionary never says how
we got from one meaning to another.

Is it too fanciful to think that Chaucer
had a hand in this transformation?
In the Middle Ages, he figured *kind*
as the Goddess Natura, who
assembled A Parliament of Fowles
(dignified birds, not fools)
to bring justice to their kind.

So, when we say *Be kind* at the end
of messages or on the bumper of our cars
are we invoking Chaucer's Goddess?
How powerful is poetry?

The Secret Life of Plants

After David Attenborough, Dylan Thomas,
Wallace Stevens

You never asked me whether I believe in God
but I'm going to tell you anyway. Not in
saviors or mothers, buddhas or fathers.
Not in any prescribed Way or Truth
although I do love the vernal or autumnal
equinox when day and night are equal,
and the Anishinaabe faith in a Great Spirit
that shares responsibility with people
and animals as sentient beings.

Yet when I see the time-lapse images
in David Attenborough's films of plants
taken on every continent, in every stressful state
--extreme heat, frozen tundra, flood, drought
excessive sunlight, near darkness--
and see the lengths to which each plant will go
to live, sometimes waiting for years under
ground for the right conditions to bloom,
then quickly depositing seed for the next cycle,
I willingly pledge allegiance to creativity itself:
the force that through the green fuse drives the flower.
The ingenuity that causes a fern
to curl around her sister to reach the sun
and a person to write poetry.

If there must be a god in the house,
let it move as plants do,
as co-creators of a livable world.

After Neruda

Trees cannot bleed,
wind cannot weep,
'though they have cause.

It is up to us to feel
the blade and cry out
against the thrust,

to cry for those
who cannot speak
for themselves

or whose languages
are still unknown,
to cry aloud

so loud that
even the deaf
can hear.

It is up to us.

Journey to the Source of the Orinoco River

Exploracion de las fuentes del rio Orinoco, 1959
A painting by *Remedios Varo*

She travels to the place of origins
in her open egg-shaped vessel
buttoned together like a coat
angel wings for sails
mere strings to hold them
fish tail for rudder
a thin line as helm

Her destination
a hollow tree
a room within
a crystal goblet
gushing the water
that will bring the forest
to its death by drowning

Black birds in nearby trees
look on as if they know the story
who put the table there
the overflowing glass.

III

Conundrums

Conundrum

In Appleton, Wisconsin, c. 1995

I'd hate to be you
a pre-school child called to my friend
who stopped her morning walk
and stepped closer to ask *Why?*

Because my mommy hates
people who look like you
the girl proclaimed from her porch
before she scampered inside.

Several minutes later when
Pat joined me to continue walking
she was reeling. She'd been stung
before but not by one so young.

What's to hate? Surely not her
natural hair or cinnamon skin!
She was an island woman with a ready
smile. We stared at each other, stunned.

Why would a Wisconsin woman
become so fixed in prejudice
that her small child would feel free
to taunt another mother?

What Troubles Me Most?

Is it the bumper sticker that says
May God grant you the wisdom
to allow me to control you

or the one that says
Every man for himself,
meaning no help or restraint?

Who are these people,
who want to control me,
or live without guardrails?

I choose neither the Ruler
who thinks he knows best,
nor the Anarchist,

rather the middle way
where people walk together
with a certain humility

knowing that no empire can
last forever and no one is free
of the need for air and water.

Today

I knew my poem would
have to be about the wind
that set the trees to swaying
several feet each way.

I didn't need to see the Lake
to know how high the waves
will be, how the season
for boating is over, how
soon we'll be hearing
of struggles to get into ports
running aground on shoals
or into rocks, pylons, docks.

So many late autumn
early-winter shipwrecks
happened over the centuries
that they seem inevitable.
The waves begin to rise
in August and continue
until the surface ices over.

But there is no law of Nature
that decrees war, is there?
Surely human tempers
can be restrained.
Who is at this Helm?

The Trouble with Democracy

which I otherwise love,
is the vigilance it requires.

How did News venues get away
with re-telling the Big Lie for years?

How did the mysterious Q-Anon elect anyone?
Wasn't the Con Man discarded with his snake oil?

One Party stands against voting fraud
which no one can find in numbers to matter

but what about fraud that makes a difference
to people just trying to live out their lives:

astronomical charges for insulin, epi-pens
to fund another private offshore bank account?

Vigilance to stop injustice takes
so much time and energy!

But without it, democracy flounders.
Like a precocious child, it needs constant attention.

Change

The interim minister says change is good. We have changed the way we do things over and over since forever, new tools, improved dwellings, better theories. Methods may alter extravagantly as long as the message at the center remains.

He thinks the message is love; I think survival. As human beings. Of the web that holds us together with all species. Love is wonderful but not always present.

Change is everywhere. Always. A basic fact of existence. But the web makes limits. Extend it too far and its threads weaken, break. Sometimes we dangle in space, waiting for it to be repaired.

Some plants bloom and bloom.
Change is good until it's not.
Death is hard to bear.

It is probably not wise

either to hope out loud
that Artificial Intelligence
with its quick and comprehensive
answers to the questions we ask
will make it harder for our voters
to be taken in by billionaires
oligarchs and demagogues--
that the sheer weight of information
will press out false histories

or to express my nagging fear
that a need to belong may win the day
with roaring crowds or mobs on fire
with strong emotions to daze the brain
and tase the body into submission
to a charismatic voice or stance
without regard to truth or facts

while news around the world suggests
that anything can happen.

On a Line from Patricia Smith

from *Blood Dazzler,* poems about *Katrina*

Every damned body needs a midnight stage

a place where the inner dam can break
a time when the dammed voice can speak

especially when the one who damns
is a force of nature, long dammed up

by others of our kind with dazzling dams
meant to save us from being damned

to death by drought, but collaterally damning
other species to extinction with dams

that stop them from spawning, damn
them to return to undammed waters

without their young, damning themselves.
Damn it, where is this infernal stage

where the dammed can express our rage?

Found Poem about the 2024 Milwaukee Convention

from Abraham J. Reisman and Heather Cox Richardson

Kayfabe is the performance aspect of professional wrestling. Actors play out scenes of good and evil, love and hate, loyalty and betrayal. In the past, their masks were not allowed to slip. The audience entered stable illusions. Later, promoters and wrestlers tossed real-life insults into the scenes. Now, *Neo-kayfabe* rests *on a slippery, ever-wobbling jumble of truths, half-truths, and outright falsehoods*, albeit delivered with passion and commitment.

> Politics becomes wrestling.
> Wrestling follows politics.
> Who will grow our food?

Pray, how would we know him?

Jesus is coming very, very soon
From a billboard in Green Bay, Wisconsin

His skin will likely be dark, and since he spoke
for the poor and lame, the hungry and sick
he may be poor himself, one of those who visits
the food pantry under the cover of night,
humble, perhaps humiliated.

We may have put him in jail
for his color or some imagined transgression
like those of his inner-city brothers.

We can hardly expect to match his DNA.
Besides, we don't trust science, unless
our hearts malfunction or melanoma forms.

Maybe he has already come and gone
without notice, say in the person
of Martin Luther King

Maybe he came as a child to our southern border
as a test of our belief in his principles
and we were found wanting.

Anyway, who's to say he would come here
rather than to, say, Jerusalem? Maybe
the poor in Africa are more deserving.

And here's the final rub: which one would come--
He who raised Lazarus from the dead, or the man
who overturned the tables in the Temple?

If We Could

One day in nursery school, I'm told,
a boy between the ages of two and five,
was sent to the corner muzzled
like a dog for biting me.

I've never known if the method
curbed his appetite for flesh,
whether he felt guilt or shame,
but he did not bite me again.

When the babies bit my nipples,
I stopped nursing, stopped
playing when our dog
or cats nipped a hand.

When a grandchild threatened
a brother with a dip in hot lava
his parents sent him from the room
to contemplate his choices.

Native nations used to exile those
who could not live in harmony,
would not settle their disputes
according to tribal customs.

What if we just bleeped all hateful
speech the way we do foul language?
Could we keep this disease
from spreading?

English As She is Spoke

How does anyone learn to sound out English
with so many overlaps and exceptions, and no one
like the French Academy to act as a final authority?
Take my husband's family name: *Lauterwasser*,
German for loud or clear or pure water, now *Lauter*.
Auf Deutsch, it would be Lao-ter, in Scotland, Lawder.
Americans often flounder or take a stab: Estee *Lauder*?
They go for a sound they've heard, preferably in public.
Do I exaggerate? Of course. But think of the black bow
tie and the bow at the end of a performance,
the bough on a tree and the beau for a lady.

It's all because the Britons were conquered by so many
--Danes, Vikings, Romans, Angles, Saxons, Normans.
The Colonies assimilated words from everywhere else.

But the person now learning English—how words sound
and how they look on a page—has no time for history.
They say it is easy: subject, verb, object, no worries
matching genders of adjectives and nouns.

It's *not* so easy.
Every culture has a stake
in this big garden of dreams.

Woke

Ebonics for "awakened"

Hey, I was there in the Seventies
when books by women, Blacks, Gays
Natives, Asians, Latinas became available
--*American* lives were laid out on the page--
and readers began to understand that
we, they, I, you were all profoundly human.

Just a fact, not an ideology
so it didn't make sense to call out
insulting names or put oneself up
and someone else down.

We saw how *language had made difference*
made it up, created it, kept it in place.

Reading of lives we hadn't known
hearing voices we hadn't heard
we saw that everyone needs respect
and thought that anyone who read
these books would feel the same.

Instead, we are accused of violating
the freedom to say whatever slur
might rise from the pit of fear.

One man's idea of freedom has become
more important than another's humanity.

Now those books are often banned
by those who know all too well
the power of words.

The Poet Considers Revolution

The day's word candy floats above the restless poet.
Today's headlines are hard candies
that pucker her brow like lemons:

Words that put the kibosh on liberty and justice for all.

Words uttered with turpitude
where one galumphing man bloviates
to flummox his followers
and mollifies them masterfully
asking them to put their lives
in abeyance, in deference to him.

Words that divide and obliviate.

The poet will be restless until
these candies are dissolved.

Weather Unavailable

says my smart phone and I think
of the sign we saw in Beijing
for a photography studio:
We Shoot Brides.
What happens there in art
must not be true in life.

Less funny is the thought
that those who favor virtual
reality might see the absence
of an internet connection as
an absence of weather itself.
No Siri: no weather.

Then there's the news this week
of temperatures above 120F
for days on end, where people
without means to cool the air will die.
No joke if the weather really
stops supporting life.

IV

Wishes

On Reconciliation

1.
Outside the city wall in Derry
is a sculpture of two men
in their prime, thin and muscular.
They stand tall but reach
toward one another
their fingers not quite touching.

2.
In Belfast, a Felon's Club is run by
and for former prisoners of The Troubles
released by the Good Friday Agreement.
A panel, one from the IRA, another
from the Orangemen and a British soldier
talk about their path from enemy to friend
with such respect, we ask how we might learn
to speak across our own notorious divide.

3.
I read the terrible history of England: Britons
conquered by Rome and then by Anglo Saxons,
Danes, Norwegian Vikings, Normans,
until they must have thought it was the way
of the world to conquer others. War after war,
back and forth across the narrow Channel
up and down the island for six hundred years,
no federal code of law, only strongmen.

4.
In Dublin, a Memorial to the Easter Rising
for Irish sovereignty takes up a city block.
At the bottom of a shallow pool lie
mosaic images of weapons, broken
cast aside, released, in a ritual gesture.

5.
If the Irish can reconcile after centuries
of oppression and nearly a hundred years
of bloody Civil War, why can't we?

6.
The national flag of Eire has three colors:
Orange for Protestant Union Loyalists
Green for Catholic Republican Independents
White in the middle for peace.

In the Epilogue to *As You Like It*

Shakespeare, whoever he was, seems so sure
that we, the members of his audience,
whomever we are, have liked his play,
wherein four couples find their mates,
though they are banished from their homes
and make their choices before they know
how they will make their living

that we, four centuries later, will like
these marriages based on love-at-first-sight
pheromones, that we will still believe in
the attraction of opposite sexes
groan when one brother tries to kill the other
applaud when they make up

that we will know the life-sustaining
value of the forest better than its dangers
(but fie on Will for putting a lion in England)

that we will value peace
and wish for order.

But all the while, the playwright
knows that whatever we may like
our lives will follow the same pattern
of seven ages on the world's stage
from mewling infant to oblivion.

Only in the play may we decide
what we like and have it.

The Law of the Great Peace

It's not the first-time grievances have risen to the point we see now in Israel and Gaza. The Haudenosaunee (Iroquois Nations) recount their own long, troubled history south of Lake Ontario in their founding story.

It begins with Hiawatha, whose entire family is killed. He goes crazy with grief and soon the whole community is in danger from his vengeance, which spreads to surrounding communities, until killing becomes the norm instead of an extreme. An unknown figure called *Peacemaker* appears and sits with this man *counting wampum,* where each bead is a grief or grievance that led to a violent response. They sit together a long time with no judgment, handling the beads until the man's anger is calmed. Then they rise and go from one nation to another to create *The Law of the Great Peace*, which brings both practical rules and symbolic rituals to the People. The process creates a Confederation, whose legislators, chosen and deposed by women Elders, learn to make decisions by consensus. Each nation buries its weapons under the great white pine that stands for peace.

The Law passes by word of mouth for generations until an alphabet for Iroquoian languages is written, and it lasts six centuries until the American Revolution, when parts of it are woven into the US Constitution. It continues to inform the hearts and minds of Haudenosaunee People.

As the Allies asked the Navajo to use their language for coded messages in World War II, might supporters of Israel and Palestine now ask Iroquois Elders to mediate the current Middle Eastern war?

> As Ireland now celebrates
> the end of its great troubles
> may we bury our weapons

Race with a Capital "R"

Let's give up the Category based on physical traits
that makes a person part of a Race, going
beyond place, ethnicity, nationality,
and sets a person up or down,
compared with members of another Race.

Race is a Mistake made long ago
like thinking the Earth is flat.
When Europeans saw dark men
they elevated color to a Category
of human being—a division by skin.

Since white meant light and goodness
and black meant moral darkness
all those with dark skin were suspect
and light became "white," each a marker
of belonging that spanned continents.

When Science couldn't find the proof of Race
in real bodies and couldn't say one group
was better than another, those who wanted
the order of opposites—white/black, good/evil
would give up neither Word nor judgment.

    It's up to us now
    to let it go, let
    it go, let it go.

Like Deer

After Jean Nordhaus

One winter I photographed
a family of five deer who were
so starved they came straight
to our deck for bird seed.

I'd see them moving slowly through
the trees, so I'd remove my shoes,
find the camera, step quietly
to the window where the light
was right that day, turn off the flash
and wait—not for great photos
through two panes of smudged glass,
but to pay enough attention, to know
the one who limped was healing,
to see the coyote looking on
and scare him away.

I wish we could see our own poor
as families whose lives are interrupted
by bad weather, whose bodies must
survive with pride. I want to say
be gentle so their beauty thrives
comes out like deer to food
or a woman to love.

Like Trees

In this new-growth forest
no one over a hundred years
trees don't mind strong winds.
Last week in storm after storm
even their trunks swayed wildly

but they stand quietly today
as if catching their breath
a few small branches at the top
flaring out in an occasional gust
as leaves below scarcely ripple.

Sturdy, but flexible. Tall, but
able to bend and reach out.
Receptive and therefore
self-sufficient, in contact
with others of their kind
but also able to let go.

Surely the Great Chain of Being
with minerals and plants
at the bottom and mankind
at the top of earthly lives
should be turned on its side
the better to value trees.

They Shall Remain

After the 2009 PBS Series, *We Shall Remain*

Now that we have established a day
each spring to remember the Holocaust
my thoughts come home to this Continent,
to all the miraculous survivals
of terrible intent.

To Cherokee women stumbling through snow,
seven states marked forever
by their bloody footprints,
and the men, burying their dead
in unmarked graves along the way.

To Ho-Chunk warriors
who hid out in Wisconsin forests
to avoid the *five* Removals
that displaced their relations
all the way to Nebraska.

To the parents who watched their children
lose their native bearings, often to lie forever
in boarding school cemeteries, and those who lost
their language when the last speaker died.
My eyes burn at how close they came to extinction.

They shall remain, along with those upon whose backs
rest American agriculture and trade,
and waves of immigrants who fled destruction
on other continents. I wish, one day
we may learn to live together in peace.

Three Wishes

Last spring, we walked below the bluff
at the end of the Door Peninsula
to see Anishinaabe images in rock:
an elk, a thunderbird and two canoes.

Signs on a map for hunters far from home,
they also served as spirit guides.
Come here, the artists said,
where your ancestors found food and power.

Even faded by sun, wind and time,
these paintings made from tough
red roots and sturgeon oil
remain on this exposed cliff.

Even now, they wish us duration—a long life
filled with rich experiences together.
Creativity—the will to make
the most of what we find.

Commitment—not just to ourselves
but to *the ones who come after.*

Touch the earth lightly, but leave
your marks so caring eyes can see them.

V.

This land is your land, this land is my land,

2004-2024

The American Grey Squirrel

He wants it all.
Mounts the rail. Too far away.
Climbs the windowsill. Too low.
Tries a nearby bough. Too wobbly.

He ponders and gathers his strength.
Aha. The corner where
those windows almost meet
looks solid, so he clambers up
hurls himself at the feeder
and falls without the slightest grace.

A minute later
he sits on the roof's edge
to peer at the object of his desire
then leaps to grab the wire,
snatching just a few seeds
before his balance fails
and he is back to ground

where he could eat his fill
if enough were only enough.

Inauguration Suite

After Mary Oliver

So this is fear

The sticker on the back of an old truck
says "Pride In Prejudice."
Ten hate groups
with Christian names in Wisconsin.
History is brutal.
I remember the films of Kennedy's
last ride, the black and white stills
of Caroline and John-John
not knowing why.

I get up to clear those images
make myself breathe
as if for childbirth
the way I did when the ER staff
yanked my ankle back into line.
In—two, three, four
Out—two, three, four.
Voices on the radio sing
of shepherds' gifts
and a fine blanket of snow
covers bare branches.

2. After 2004

There was no choice
no rest, only brief sails
moments with small children
hours with poetry or music
to remind me why it was still worthwhile

to fight the tide with so little hope
it would fit on a slip of paper in a bottle.

But out of the debris came other workers
determined not to lose the whole ship
not to let ourselves be brushed down
the scuppers or shunted into lifeboats.

So we resolved, re-tooled, re-framed until we found
the candidates more likely to think first of others
and the margins folded into the center of hope.

3. November 4, 2008

Night fell.
The darkness was thin,
Streetlamps and dock lights
doubled the town's peaceful size
on the water, calm,
as if it had just been poured into the bay
to buoy our enlarging hearts.

4. January 20, 2009

After the new shock and awe,
the interviews, appointments,
speculations and pronouncements,
in anticipation of the pledge,
the hand on the book, the speech,
we wonder about the scope
of the rot and the remedies.

A black brother says we should think
not how this man can save us
but how we can save him.
And it is true
his most repeated words are

I can't do this alone, without you,
meaning not just during the campaign,
but for the duration of government
of, by and for the people.

If the country hoped
to get off the hook of democracy
it will have to learn
to hope for other things
not more or best
but goods designed to last
hundreds of years.

Return of the Marlboro Man I

Except for a few old billboards
showing the man tan and fit
on horseback, he's gone
from the world of slick ads,

replaced by computer geeks
and geckos selling insurance,
his signature brand confined
to shelves behind the counter,

the package warning that
smoking is bad for your health.
But he's making a comeback
wrapped in campaign rhetoric,

his stoic visage transformed
by anger at having to pay
for health insurance because
he's never had cancer or a pain

that couldn't be cured by alcohol
or Ibuprofen so why should
the government interfere?
Problem is, his aging mom needs

Social Security and Medicare.
His dad's a vet with benefits,
and one of the grandparents came
here to escape from European wars.

Besides, he loves to ski off-trail
in the Parks, and if a freak storm hit

because of that fake climate change,
a federal helicopter will rescue him.

The Return of the Marlboro Man II

Ever since smoking became lethal instead of cool
he's disappeared from his billboard, with his hat
and horse, wide open spaces, confident gaze.

Sure, he returned briefly for the Koch's Tea Party
but what good would it do for ALEC to rewrite
states' laws from cradle to grave if he didn't
want to be subject to any of them himself?
So when someone came along who thumbed
his nose at laws, he rallied. Oh how good it felt
to be among men like him and women who
accepted being Adam's Rib, to enjoy the praise
of pastors so the cause of absolute Freedom
could seem to be a Second Coming of the Lord.

Wahooo! The light, grown-up shirt, cigarette
and leather vest, followed by Tees with
in-your-face slogans, baggy-pants and tattoos
gave way to Red Hats and Red Shirts. A uniform
to rival Black Shirts and Brownshirts in the Thirties.

Though he hasn't yet targeted neighbors
just for being Democrats, his candidates
say that Lefties are the enemy of Freedom.
And women who refuse to bear a child need
to be taught a lesson, along with boys who
might choose not to become men. No way.
In half a century, he's gone from loss
of smokes to preparation for war with those
who refuse to give up their freedoms for his.

But the nagging problem remains. Some events
are more than anyone can handle by himself
or with a little help from his friends. Every year
wildfires, floods, droughts, tornados, hurricanes
extremes of all kinds around the globe prove
how vulnerable we humans are, how much
we need each other and those guardrails
that protect us from irreparable harm.

The American National Character

Going
    away
    around the block
    somewhere, anywhere
    from place to place
    West
    to the Moon, or Mars
    under anesthetic
    through the mill
    great guns
    crazy
Going to
    get with the plan
    see the light
    feel the burn
    do something big
    be better than
    go for broke
Going
    going, gone to the highest bidder

It Did Happen Here, U.S.A 2016

After Sinclair Lewis

The press did not question
the candidates deeply
so they became peddlers
while reporters played
at being paparazzi

The press did not investigate
as *he said* or *she said,*
so opposites sat
unexamined on the table
as if truth had ceased to exist

The press did not illuminate
repeating campaign claims
without clarification,
currying favor
to serve the bottom line

The press did not step up
to defend Common Sense
did not seek facts of debts,
foreign influence, transgressions
until after the vote was taken

and a nation stepped back, but not into greatness.

Didn't it just give you the collywobbles

when that orange dude was elected president?
I've had a doozy of a case of hives ever since
he skulked onstage to stalk Hillary Clinton.
All those snarky jabs and gunky arguments
coming after the news of his hanky-panky
left me flabbergasted. If I'd had a didgeridoo
I would have played a dirge. As it was, I gained
ten pounds eating hushpuppies and blubbered
for the first time in decades. Who did this?
It's like setting a fancy table with sporks!

November 9, 2016

This afternoon, I drove to Sven's Panorama to watch the water in Green Bay, the wind and current too strong for small crafts. All the buoys have been removed for the season—not to be crushed by ice. That is power!

To the Magas who voted yesterday: I get it. You wanted revenge, but what will you do with it? I am one of those nasty women who just wants a fair share for everyone. Should I fear you now?

To the Greens and Libertarians: the perfect is the enemy of the good.

To those who dreamed the impossible dream—a woman as President–hang in there. The buoys go back in the water each spring. In winter, even a captain familiar with his charts can run aground without these tangible reminders of rocks.

Cirrus clouds sit high
in the sky like a giant tent
coexisting with contrails.

An Elegy for Democracy

We thought we'd made the whole world
safe for democracy, if not in the Great Wars
then surely in the fall of Communism,
the triumph of free markets,
the reach of social media

so we didn't pay attention
when the large, new class
of billionaires bought
Representatives, Courts, Media
and tampered with the right to vote.

We didn't connect the dots
between think tanks for one-party rule
and guns concealed in jackets and purses
the better to shoot one who disagrees
or isn't from the neighborhood.

The men who made their fortunes
in spite of the New Deal want more
not seeing where the greed for power
led in other lands, reviling history.
They would destroy all our pillars.

Resist, we say, and millions do
but if democracy fails, it will not
matter what the people want.
The guns will be directed by
and for the wealthiest men alive.

Distress Signal

It had not occurred to her
that her country might die in its adolescence.

Though some parts of its history
gave her a hammering migraine

she had never begrudged its extravagant childhood
dappled with high adventure and smudged with mud

no better or worse than most other countries.
But after the last election, she began to fear for its life

as one after another of its bones were recklessly broken
while feverish fires raged, floods rose, and the God

from whom everyone expected a blessing
stayed well out of earshot. She needed

a bigger voice, a bagpipe, a means
to be heard above the uproar of emotion.

And on the Eighth Day, the Governor Said

Let there be no zombie studies, only classics.

And his staff searched everywhere but could not find such a thing to destroy.

They found instead a classic poem by Alexander Pope that said "The Proper Study of Mankind is Man."

But they wondered *which man*?
Confucian, Taoist, Hindu, Buddhist, Jew, Christian, Muslim?

How ancient the study--the first footsteps found in East Africa?

How modern—Martin Luther King?

And what about Woman (or women)? Children? Shall they be included?

And Robots, for surely they shall inherit the earth.

Wait! Maybe the citizens *should* study zombies,
for did not the Third Reich create a nation of followers,
bitten by desire to win without thinking?

Let's not have that.

Letter to the Editor

In my free travels around our County
I see signs that say *Fight for Freedom*

and I wonder what it means to be free.
For centuries now, we have had freedom

from rule by a king who was free to tax us
and we have fought for freedom from slavery.

We are free to vote for representatives
to make or change laws regarding freedoms

which can make us less free, as when
the need for reproductive freedom collides

with religion. But wait! We are supposedly free
from religious dogma, a freedom built into our

Constitution, free as many countries are not
to think and speak our minds with freedom

from punishment, but not free to break the law
made by our representatives. Freedom from them

requires free elections, accountability, impeachment.
But total freedom, as Berbers in the desert, is not

possible in a land of states connected by freeways
electric grids, waterways. Freedom here depends on

good government to keep our systems free from harm
by bad actors or states whose freedoms do not

match our own. Might we *feel* more free if we saw that
elsewhere people still fight for the freedoms we have?

As Thomas Paine said in 1776, in free countries only the law is King. Let freedom continue to reign.

If I tell you that I am a loyal American

but I don't believe my country
is always right, will you put me
in jail? Place a *Traitor* sign
on my lawn? I hope not
because everyone makes mistakes.
White hats, like all others, collect dirt.

Counting an enslaved man as 3/5
of a person? No way that passes
any moral test. Removing Indians
from their homes so land could
be re-distributed to settlers?
Inhumane by any standard
though sanctioned by a Pope.
Weapons of Mass Destruction
in Iraq? A President only wished.

Not to admit wrongdoing
is a tripping hazard
that becomes more serious
the longer it remains in place.

Here We Are on the Brink, 2024

Just over one hundred years
after the Treaty of Versailles
drew impossible borders

Not quite one hundred years
after Hitler's brown shirts
muscled into power

Not quite one hundred years
after the fantasy of Aryan
purity took hold

Not quite one hundred years
after so-called undesirables
were shunted into camps

Not quite one hundred years
after the Great War gave way
to a second conflagration

Here we are on the brink.

VI

A World Beyond
Our Borders

Americans Abroad

1. Lake Como, 1964

We were used to camping American-style,
on carefully cleared sites separated by trees
for privacy, but we were determined
to follow *Europe on Five Dollars a Day*
so we acclimated to noisy nights on open
grounds of crumbling estates in cities
with easy access to art and culture.

But we also relished a retreat
from that scene to Lake Como
with its deep water and high peaks.
Here we could share the heady view
that once belonged only to nobles
and follow Shelley's footsteps
along the famous walking paths.

Our homemade tent sagged
among taut European models,
but we finally began to relax
beyond the constant urban bustle,
loving the sounds of many languages
when we used the common sinks
for washing dishes, brushing teeth,
even daring to speak a few words.

We also locked the keys inside our new
VW convertible and didn't discover our blunder
until Sunday, could not remember the words
for *keys* or *help* in schoolroom French
or German. Italian was beyond the pale.

But fellow campers had been watching us.
Soon a sympathetic man began to gesture

and another called a locksmith,
who came to us instead of church or coffee.
When he opened our car door, everyone cheered.

2. West Germany, 1986

That year in Kassel we had a short-wave
radio and cringed one day to hear that
two-hundred-seventy-seven bombs killed
forty-five Libyan soldiers or officials
and fifteen civilians in ten minutes,
the wounded not yet counted.
There was no doubt about the source.
Reagan had ordered them as payback
for a Libyan attack that killed two
Americans in a Berlin discotheque.

The U.S. cast a long shadow.
From language class with Middle
Eastern immigrants, we knew how much
our cowboy policies were hated.

That day, when we dressed to bike in the city
we chose dull colors for cover,
spoke as little as possible.

But we had only to ask
for a *brotchen*
and everyone knew
who we were.
The shadow fell across our faces.

3. Western Siberia, 2006

As the only Americans except the two
black-suited Mormon missionaries in
Kurgan, a closed city before *Glasnost*,

we were always well-received
in homes for soul food and song.
Children came to practice English
where we sat talking with friends
in a public park on our way back
to our host family's high rise flat.

The main spring holiday, May 9th,
not only marked the crushing losses
of World War II, but also the first
meeting with American Allies at the Elbe.
Decorated veterans spoke with tears
about our partnership in victory
over the greatest threat they had
ever known to their security.
No talk of Cold War animosities.

But men in offices struggling to make sense
of runaway profits in wild capitalism
were less than sanguine about ideas
we carried from their Sister City in the USA.
Conversations quickly turned to history.

Didn't you learn anything from Viet Nam?
Didn't you watch us in Afghanistan?

4. 2024

The energy that once
was so attractive in Americans
seems reckless to our allies now.
Good will from the Great Wars
mostly spent.

Reading War

Coming of age in the Sixties when studying history still meant acknowledging Great Men and their achievements as Statesmen, Warriors, Judges who contributed to Human Progress, I could not have imagined myself reading novels or bios about war in retirement. I just wanted it to disappear.

Now nothing in the Twentieth Century seems more important than the two World Wars, from which we've never recovered, although they barely touched our shores. The first resulted in widespread disruptions of borders, upsetting ethnic and cultural bonds that grounded identities. The second raised profound questions about what it means to be human, if a civilized nation like Germany could be so quickly persuaded of the need for land and a concept of Race to permit genocide against longtime neighbors.

We said, *No, Never again!*
Now it's *Déjà vu.*
We long for Voltaire's Garden.

After Reading Tim O'Brien

In the Lake of the Woods

Here is how it happens
the loss of peace.

A man sees terrible things
innocent lives reduced
to pulp by youth whose nerves
are strung on instruments of death.
A cane appears to be a gun
and suddenly a grandfather lies dead.
A voice startles from above
and suddenly a buddy topples
into a pit of bodies.

But the worst part of this script,
the stickler that keeps the shooter up
some part of every night thereafter,
sends him around in a dizzying circuit,
is that he can't tell *anyone* the truth,
not even himself, lest he destroy
another life.   His own.

Speech, not sleep with its recurring dreams,
might have *knit the raveled sleeve of care*
but he has the right to remain silent
and soon he knows neither
what he did nor who he is.

These are the *spoils of war*.

Mexico City, 1983

Scrumptious food from every region
and peals of laughter late at night

An Olmec sculpture towers outside
a great museum like a Sphinx

Frida Kahlo's Blue House in Coyoacan
is full of *retablos* and brilliant *ceramica*

Classes of excited children study
paintings by the late Remedios Varo

I have rich *café solo* and chocolate
at the artist's home and studio

Talk of art and politics switches
languages back and forth, midsentence

Neruda devotees read his poems
to a crowd in the National Stadium

Stark Aztec ruins in the center city
remind me of how cultures lose power

My friend slips off-duty for a lavish meal
through the back seat of a Presidential limo

Why had so little except poverty, *frijoles*
and bad air ever been mentioned to me?

All Roads Lead to Baghdad

Day by day, we are moving closer to Baghdad
Day by day we are moving closer to victory.
George W. Bush, March 31, 2003

No matter which road our soldiers took
to this round city that burst its walls
a thousand years ago, they passed through
Mesopotamia, the Fertile Crescent, land of milk
and honey, home of the world's first cities,
oldest writing, the first legal codes, royal
tombs of Ur, Hanging Gardens of Babylon,
clay tablets of first steps toward geometry.
Here the father of three faiths was told, *by you*
all families of the earth will bless themselves.

Behind their high-tech infra-red goggles
our soldiers lined up in hundreds of trucks
and aimed their powerful weapons: bullseye
thousands of people gone. To ease the pain,
our leaders said *war is messy . . . stuff happens,*
but the cause is freedom; no sacrifice too great.
We will spread it everywhere, for *we* are
the mighty and blessed sons of Abraham.

Beyond the inky blacks and eerie colors
of those lenses, we may remember the tale
of Arabian Nights and see women, desperate
for the lives of loved ones. What stories
could they tell to satisfy this new ruler?
How many children would they give
him in his prisons, barracks, schools
and councils? Must they wait in silence
only to see Ala-al-Din's lamp go dark?

While our leader danced in his cowboy boots
after our own flawed election, I dreamt
of the man who held his brother's severed hand
and heard once more his sorrowful cry
Is this your liberation
your democracy
your freedom?

Gaza, January 2009

In seven years, we've got a whole new body.
Li-Young Lee, *Breaking the Alabaster Jar*

A European doctor on emergency duty in Gaza
says it's like being bombed in a cage,

and I think of how it must seem
to those already hospitalized
with wounds that may never heal
to hear the wham and whistle
smash and screech of missiles,
the rumble of earth giving way
as they lie immobilized
waiting for medicine.

Even the body of a patient lying quietly,
incarcerated, on life support,
generates three billion cells a minute.
In seven years, he could have a whole new body,
not as it was but *brimming* with life.

Where is Joseph, whose dreams saved
both Egyptians and the brothers who betrayed him?

Water brims to the top of a tube and trembles there.

ESTELLA LAUTER

Cri de Coeur

How will our hosts, the family
with whom we lived so happily
for three months eighteen years ago
Igor, Tanya, Yevgeny (Genya), Elena
live in Russia after this war is over?

Igor's family was Ukrainian.
Tanya's was Tatar. Now
Ukrainians are called *Nazis* in Moscow
subject to *re-education*. Tatars
are *removed* from occupied Crimea.

Where will they go?
Will Igor and Tanya be sent to separate
camps, or will their entrepreneurial success
in the Nineties provide protection
from their heritage--make them useful?

Will Genya and Elena, now in their thirties
graduates of Moscow's best university
be spared, or will their history with us
as participants in a Sister City
blot their record?

Tanya said she felt closer to us
than to her blood relatives
because of our conversations
over strong tea with jam
even in translation.

Genya lived with us one summer
and later took an unlikely job in Africa.
With her excellent education, did Elena
marry or rebel, stay in Moscow
under Putin's thumb, or leave?

Our hope of ever hearing from them dims
in direct proportion to news of Russia's war.

History

*Men and death, Men and death. How on earth y'all run
the world when all y'all ever done is kill each other?*
Tara Stringfellow, *Memphis.*

Words spoken by a Black woman in a novel by a Black
American woman, but they reverberate on this day
the one-year mark in Russia's illegal war on Ukraine
a time when every ounce of our creative energy is
needed to counter a stronger enemy: climate change.

The woman pleads
for the life of her son
convicted of murder
about to be sentenced.
It is one thing to perish in a storm
quite another to die as part
of an endless cycle of killing.

This war, a clear abrogation of laws
already broken by the Third Reich
in the name of Aryan purity
is fueled once more by desire
for the ultimate power to bring
about the death of others.

I wear the blue and yellow
stand against electric chairs.
Pray for human survival.

The Road to Hell Is Paved

A nation is threatened by a terrorist strike.
It decides to destroy individual terrorists
saying it can do so according to law.

Another nation deemed essential
to the survival of worldwide democracy
has a history of wars against terrorism.
It warns against repeating its mistakes
but still agrees to fund a ground war
along with its opposite, humanitarian
supplies for innocents in that war.

But it proves *impossible* for trucks
to bring *enough* water, food and medicines
for two million people under constant fire.

Impossible for a ground war *not*
to kill innocent people in a place
where so many live packed like sardines.

Impossible to evacuate
when roads are bombed
and there is no safe place to go.

Impossible to resolve such tensions
born of a hundred years of wars
without talking together.

Dante knew
where this road leads
when human emotion exceeds what is possible.

Untitled

How to register profound dismay
not to mention fear and alarm
at the decision to perpetuate
war in Gaza through Ramadan

a war doomed to fail
at wiping out Hamas
since it is neither a place
nor a state, but an alliance
formed in response to decades
of encroachment through fences
illegal settlements and walls
above all, walls, that stop
the daily bread from coming in
and workers from reaching their fields.

Areas designated for Palestinians
are patrolled by Israeli soldiers.
Now, miles of rubble are bombed
over and over in a vain attempt
to kill every member of Hamas
without killing innocent Palestinians.

The irony of bombing during Ramadan
a time when Muslims contemplate
charity, is lost to the Western world
where the Qu-ran's music is rarely heard.

Thou Shalt Not Kill

Two wrongs do not make right.
Eye for eye, tooth for tooth, not right.
No matter who did what first, it's still not right.
Even when survival is at stake, the killing can't be right.
Capital punishment by the state and by law is also not right.
Survival of all species depends on telling what's wrong from right.
What a mess we've made of this Commandment!   Make it right?

Reflection
on Octavia Butler's
Parable of the Sower

In the Nineties she foresaw a time
—the 2020s—under conservative rule
when laws would turn against most citizens
and gated communities would be burned
by those without food and shelter
living on one drug or another

a time when new seeds would be sown
new lands found to nurture them
unsettled lands with enough water
not too much heat and freedom
to read, write, think outside the box
—the hero, Lauren, thinks of stars

planets in our universe or another
where a small group of humans
might begin again--repeating the cycle
of death and rebirth, Sodom and Gamora
revised in a foreign land of fruit and honey
with love, at least respect, for one another

and I think of current headlines in our news
where teachers in Florida have to hide their books
for fear of prison, mass shootings happen every week
and Elon Musk takes super-wealthy tourists out in space.

If we can't live in peace here
let's not take our beastly troubles to the moon!

Picking Rocks

When we first came to this peninsula
between Lake Michigan and Green Bay
the farmers told us how they'd
cleared the land as kids, pulled the rocks
out of soil after they'd splintered from
their limestone bed each winter
and heaved to the surface in what
seemed an endless process
--a childhood filled with stones
that families used for walls
to mark their boundaries.

Now, fifty years later, each spring
I find more rocks pushing up
as if they wanted to be noticed
like wildflowers, in shades of white
and grey with streaks of rust
fossils, folds, layers and breaks
to tell us where they've been
and what they have stored.

I pick them carefully, keeping their moss
place them around our flower beds.
Ours is not the only history
that deserves remembering.

The Universe and Us

Ashes to ashes and dust to dust
but don't forget the gases--
hydrogen, helium, traces of carbon,
in our cauldron, our star womb.

Don't forget about the gases
expanding then cooling
in our cauldron, our star womb,
as gravity pulls in,

expanding then cooling
clouds, nebulae, star cocoons,
as gravity pulls in
factories for cells.

Clouds, nebulae, star cocoons
seed the elements around and within,
make factories for cells
planets, mountains, people

our brothers, our sisters.
Hydrogen, helium, traces of carbon
are burning, cooling, seeding, pulling
ashes to ashes, dust to dust.

VII

Do We Still
Believe
in Miracles?

Miracles

It's a miracle, we say,
when a father of three
survives a terrible accident
and lives into his eighties
like Lazarus rising from the dead.

Then how much more miraculous
it is when out of all the gases
of our star, two molecules
of hydrogen bonded with one
of oxygen to make water

in its myriad forms, ice, snow
frazil, foam, mist or steam,
but surely the greatest
is the liquid that carries
food to nourish cells

in all the bodies on our planet
animal and plant. It streams
through passages so small
as to seem invisible. But
there's a catch: it must be fresh

for most of us who live
on land, untainted by salts
or acids. We need another
miracle, we say, and we
still believe in miracles.

Water, Water, Everywhere, but . . .

Soon we may see ships
pulling giant balloons
of fresh water along
all our coasts,

multi-storied
greenhouses and pink
light to grow
our food in deserts,

nuclear fusion to power
desalination,
an unknown planet
with vast supplies of H2O,

whole populations
becoming water nomads
moving to places like Great
Bear Lake in Canada.

If not,
what then?
A teacher once told me
that poets answer questions.
Maybe not.

Ankle-deep in Earth

Appleton, WI, circa 1970

Almost thirty before I had a garden of my own
I didn't recognize the plants I had inherited
with our midwestern university house

so, at the end of spring, wanting to ground
myself in this flat land, a thousand miles
west from home
               I pitchforked the center
of the plot that stretched the width
of our lot, upending sturdy Hostas
and other timeless staples

wading in its rich soil
relishing the feel of moist clumps
as they fell apart under my feet

before I planted roses
to remind me of eastern landscapes
though home was never more
than a figure of my imagination.

I did not know then, never having
visited a desert or lived on bedrock
how lucky I was to play in soil
so deep, how frivolous it would
later seem to plant these dressy
ornamentals instead of food.

131 Years
of Global Warming
in 26 Seconds

From the video on *YouTube*

Imagine a world map all in blue,
a cool color chosen for the average
global temperature in 1880.

Then watch as filaments of white
flicker over oceans and spots of yellow
shimmer and shift on several lands. Look,
you can see our Dust Bowl forming
in the Thirties as yellow darkens
to gold or copper, and the Arctic
begins to look like rust. There's a flash
of bronze from Antarctica in the Fifties.
By the Eighties the warmer hues
stretch out *en masse*, spreading further
through the Nineties, quickly turning
the map brown with a crown of blood.
By 2011, only a few small patches
 of blue remain over our oceans.

Children look stunned
when they see how a rise
of only 1.5 degrees

has affected the atmosphere
of Planet Earth, how the colors
of fire engulf our world.

So much depends on

the fungi among us
the yeasts and molds
that feed on debris
(alive or dead)
and reproduce by spores
not sex or photosynthesis

the mushrooms that grow
on forest trees like graceful
pagodas, those many-tiered
temples that shelter both
Asian gods and the Buddha
who does not claim divinity

for they will inherit the earth
as we depart, reduced to matter,
food for a separate kingdom,
a brave new world
made from neither
animal nor plant.

What's the Point?

the Astronomer asks in a new play
after her husband's fatal heart attack.

She has devoted her life to science
placing knowledge at the pinnacle
always believing that whatever is
*un*known will be known one day.

She wants to hear her husband's
voice and know if he still lives
in another world, something
science cannot tell her yet.

Survival. Isn't that the point?
If not here in body, then somewhere
in some form, maybe on the page
or simply in the minds of others.

I think of our time in the Serengeti
how a tribe of monkeys in a tree
overlooking a valley saw the lion
crouching in tall grass and sounded

an alarm that carried to the far side
where a small herd of antelope grazed
and they immediately took off, full speed
leaving the lion well behind.

We care, not just about our own
survival but that of others, not just
our species but as many as
our minds can hold in trust.

We live to continue life itself.

Desire

We wanted to see a glacier
and the Mendenhall near Juneau
still presents a thick expanse of ice
with a classic blue face, untold numbers
of crevasses in a deeper blue
and black streaks
where ice has scraped rock
when its weight moved
the massive structure down
to calve at sea level
its silt turning the water grey-green.

Salmon swim here to lay their eggs
in this cloudy water that forms new streams.
Hundreds of people come each day
all spellbound.

Still photos over fifty years
show how much has vanished.
No one can fail to see it.
Too much.
Too fast.

It will not return.

Antarctica

Aside from the images of penguin fathers
sitting on eggs and warming their young on their feet

and stories of the brave explorers
who sought to raise a flag on the South Pole

and chapters from *The Ministry for the Future*
where melting is slowed by ingenious scientists

I confess a lifelong ignorance about Antarctica. It was
just a continent, larger than Europe and Australia, ho hum.

But since our daughter traveled to an island research center
as a guest of the Chilean government conference on the future

I am agog. Under ice, the world's tallest mountains,
over a hundred volcanoes. The coldest and driest place

on earth, where fish and birds, whales and krill,
six kinds of seals and fifteen kinds of penguins

have adapted to survive for eons. One age of exploration
is over. Another has begun. No point in planting flags

if the seas will simply cover them, so men and women
from every other continent come to study the past,

present and future of our world, all the kingdoms,
weather and climate, stars and planets. A continent

dedicated to peaceful purposes and secrets of survival.
Nothing ordinary about it.

I'm Not Asking
for the Moon

or a virtuoso healer
not even a diva
to sing the praises of peace,
just a few creative ideas
to let the earth's billions live together
without brandishing words and instruments
of mass destruction.

Open the louvres of young minds
to a cooperative
not a corporate world.

Unmoor ourselves from money.

Become backyard gardeners to forestall
the coming battles over land and water.

Tend to the marrow of life
instead of its voluptuous surface.

Draw us into the circle
of the Great Spirit
that requires all
animals, plants, minerals alike
to continue the act of creation.

Maybe I am
asking for the moon.

VIII

Looking for a place to set another anchor

Adrift

You ask what this stage of life is like
and I say that while we are still allied with
family and friends, some near, some far,
and care about our country even in its
un-hinged state, we feel unmoored.

We move gingerly from port to port
looking for a place to dock or set another
anchor—midwestern charm undone
by fear and hate, more like the South
still fighting its uncivil war.

Our sense of purpose
shrouded in fog

no wind to sail
no port calling

we hunker down to wait
for better light.

Still Life Reviving

Naturaleza Muerta Resucitardo, 1963,
was Remedios Varo's last finished painting
and the only one that had no people in it.

Instead of nature
stilled for painting
perpetual motion
around candlelight

the tablecloth is
gathering force
plates flying

some fruits
rise and rotate
like planets

    apple, lemon, lime,
    orange, peach, pear
    plum, pomegranate
    strawberry

while others smash
releasing seeds
that sprout roots
bring forth buds
so the earth
shall not perish
although
we humans
do our best
to devour it

no one left
to witness
except
dragonflies.

Meditation on Snowshoes

My shoes crunch in Easter snow
a slow beat without a quiver
while thought festers around a sliver:
the sound of Gandhi walking so,
leading his people down to their own
sea to harvest their own salt and deliver
a message that made England shiver
to think what the Crown would forego.

Where now is our Gandhi-ji?
Half the world's children are still
without food, shelter and water,
protection from slaughter.
Who among us has the will
to work this sliver free?

Silence

I think of it as healing
quietness for contemplation
turning inward, letting go
of worry and intention

but my husband tells a story
about another kind of silence
when students at his university
completely filled the Chapel
where Gov. George Wallace
was to speak in 1972.

They arrived early, *en masse*
precluding others from attending
and there they sat in silence
for the music meant to stir them,
the speaker's wife who tried
to bring them into a political fold
and the man himself, who hoped
to sell them white supremacy.

Partway into his prepared speech
the front row of students
all Black, got up and walked
up the aisle single file
to the chapel doors, *and they
never said a mumbling word.*

My husband said it was the most
effective protest he ever witnessed.

And I, who had not thought of silence
as an outward motion
wonder what other means of protest
I might have missed.

Seeing the Moon

as a test case for *life* outside our planet
yardstick of mankind's prowess
proving ground in a Cold War
escape hatch for improvident earthlings
is a mistake with serious implications.

It's been fifty years since the Moon Walk
and the iconic photo of our Blue World
without much progress on the ground
or the seas, in learning *how to live*
what to do with what we have on Earth.

It's getting harder to remember the moon
as the puller of tides or measurer of months
to revere its goddesses and connect our
hemispheres--harder to feel awe
at something larger than ourselves.

Enough tramping on the moon.
Trample Mars as you will but defend
our moon from human development.
Keep it as a symbol of love, mystery, beauty
a reminder of how much we need the light.

Endangered Species

Like the two-toed sloth, I am hanging on
to hope that our young nation will not fail
to find its footing once again after recent
blows to its form and spirit.

Hope thrives on the leaves of history that show
astonishing recoveries from grand misrule,
as in the folktale of an Emperor's imaginary
clothes, which likely had its origin in facts.

When I saw the wild sloth in Costa Rica
tucked in among the branches of a giant tree
I marveled at its stillness and solidity.
Its claws will not let go even if it is shot.

I, too, am slow to anger, steady
in dark times, determined not to let go
of values that have sustained good lives.
As long as time does not run out, we will survive.

Still The Thing With Feathers

After Emily Dickinson, 2020

Hope is the Ruby-throated
Hummingbird who comes
mid-May to look for food
where it had been last fall.

His faded feeder is not
yet there, so he checks
the seed and suet, then flies
into the greening leaves.

Within the hour, my mate
inside prepares the sugared
water in its sterile bottle
to tide him over to the flowers.

We wait, not patiently,
but sure enough, a day
later he comes again
flying straight to the right

spot and perching there
for a long comforting drink
of nectar. Then, the very
next day, there are two.

Turning Back to Earth

The ones who came to these shores
on the first ships, seeking freedom
to worship or release from worn-out
loyalties, decided *not* to turn

to Earth for guidance, to a Great Spirit
that did not require offerings of gold
or altars to make its presence known.
They could have learned how to move

with the seasons, to plant in cycles,
eat only the plentiful game and fish,
live with the land and be satisfied
with *enough*, not always seeking *more*.

They could have learned to live within
a web of life where all are not exactly
equal but each one plays a valued role
that is not lightly overruled.

The Earth remains, not quite intact
but quivering with light we could still share.

And Then There's Monkey Business

After Rev. Scott Alexander

Our friend told a story about the first golf course in Calcutta. The Brits soon found that it presented an unanticipated problem. The monkeys loved golf balls. If a ball landed in the rough, they would move it to the fairway. If it was a perfect shot, they would move it to the rough. The owners tried everything from fences and removals to sprays with no success. They finally decided that the ball would be played from wherever the monkeys put it.

Climate change is here
It is not a game
Think seven generations

Epilogue:

Politics

Politics makes the world go around.
It's always present as a seed
but it often stays underground.

We govern our world in ways profound
as we work each day at breakneck speed.
Politics makes the world go around.

We prefer to use ideas just found
(belief in newness is our creed)
but they often come from underground.

We try so hard to shut it down
as if on our own we could succeed
but politics makes the world go around.

It's how we arrange things to surround
ourselves and loved ones with what we need
even when hidden underground.

When you want to toss it on a burial mound
consider carefully what you cede.
Politics makes the world go around
but it often lives on underground.

NOTES ON THE POEMS

Epigraph: "Peter Piper": This poem was the inspiration for the book, as the author considered how Peter would pick *pickled* peppers in this tongue twister. It came out of nowhere in a "free-write" led by Robin Chapman at Bjorklunden (Baileys Harbor, WI), and one p-word led to another.

"Personification . . .": Layly Longsoldier is known for her defense of the sentence in poetry. Her best-known poem is "38," about the Native men who were hanged in Mankato, MN on orders from President Lincoln in 1863.

"The Secret Life of Plants": The italicized lines are quotations from Dylan Thomas and Wallace Stevens. Attenborough's film, *The Secret Life of Plants*, presents plants in slow motion (over hours, days, weeks) to show how active and creative they are.

"Found Poem . . .": The words were found in Heather Cox Richardson's daily "Letters from An American" archived in heathercoxrichardson@substack.com.

"Americans Abroad, III Western Siberia, 2006": The author participated in a Sister City Program between the Fox Cities, WI and Kurgan, Russia, which lasted 25 years, from 1990 until 2015, when V. Putin declared all NGOs were agents of a foreign (enemy) nation.

"What's the Point?" comes from a new play by Sean Grennan, *A Rock Sails By*, premiered by Peninsula Players (Fish Creek, WI) in 2023.

"Silence": "he never said a mumbling word" is from an African American spiritual about the courage that African slaves learned from the life of Jesus. It was made famous by Lead Belly and was part of the Civil Rights Movement in the US.

Epilogue: "Politics": In responding to the assignment of a villanelle in a class by Marilyn Taylor at Bjorklunden (Baileys Harbor, WI), the author found that politics pops up from the past where and when one might least expect it, thereby derailing our attempts to control or even to understand it fully. It was a humbling experience.

Acknowledgements:

Thanks to the editors of the presses, anthologies, journals and web sites who have published previous versions of these poems

Bramble: *Peter Piper* (2nd prize in Wisconsin Writers Association Jade Ring contest); *On Reconciliation*

Echolocations: Poets Map Madison: Sarah Busse, Shoshauna Shy, and Wendy Vardaman, Eds. Cowfeather Press: *Maya Angelou in the Union Theater, 1990*

Finishing Line Press for selections from the author's books: *Incubator, That Craggy Line, The Universe and Us; Celestial Pablum, Journey to the Source of the Orinoco River, Still Life Reviving; Here We Are On the Brink.*

Free Verse: *The American Grey Squirrel.*

Hope Is the Thing, Wisconsin Historical Society Press: *Still the Thing with Feathers*

No Breath Is Lost, The Dickinson Series, I, UU Fellowship, Ephraim: *They Shall Remain*

No More Can Fit Into the Evening, Thomas Davis and Standing Feather, Eds. Four Windows Press: *Incubator, Pray Tell, How Would We Know Him? The Poems of Our Climate, Peter Piper, Belief.*

Soundings: Door County in Poetry: Caravaggio Press: *Three Wishes*

The Nature of Door Norbert Hill and Karen Yancy, eds., Cross Roads Press: *Three Wishes*

The Peninsula Pulse: *Incubator* (1ˢᵗ in the Grutzmacher contest); *All Roads Lead to Baghdad* (2ⁿᵈ prize); *The Secret Life of Plants* (3ʳᵈ prize); *Is That All There Is?* (Honorable mention), *Dear Saint Joan, On a Line from Patricia Smith* (Honorable mention).

Verse Wisconsin: *Like Deer*

What Is Hidden, The Dickinson Series, IV, UU Fellowship, Ephraim, WI: *A Poet Asks Why I Write Political Poems.*

Wisconsin Fellowship Of Poets Calendars: *After Neruda (2018), Conundrum (2019), Meditation on Snowshoes (2012), Shadow Woman (2016)*

www.wagingpeace.org: *Gaza, 2009* (tied for first prize in the 2009 Barbra Mandigo Kelly Peace Poetry Contest).

Thanks also to Chuck Lauter, Chera Van Falcon Burg, Tom and Ethel Davis, Don and Barbara Fuhrmann, Annette Grunseth, Sharon Auberle and Ralph Murre for reading versions of the manuscript and offering good advice, and to our daughter Kristin Lauter for her encouragement to finish the book. Without Chuck's support for my writing, there would be no books.

I am grateful for the opportunity to be published by Four Windows Press.

ABOUT THE AUTHOR

Estella Lauter began to understand everyday politics when, as a child, she moved every year or two up and down the East Coast from Massachusetts to Florida. Educated at the Northfield School and the University of Rochester (BA and PhD), she taught at Rochester and Lawrence University before joining the faculty at the University of Wisconsin Green Bay (1971) and later, the University of Wisconsin Oshkosh, where she became Professor Emerita in 2003. She was an Exchange Professor at the Universitaet Kassel in West Germany in 1985-86, and a Visiting Professor at Kurgan State University in Russia in 2006.

As a founder of programs in Women's Studies and American Indian Studies, she became aware of university politics, but she did not begin to study American electoral politics until, in retirement, she became an officer in the local Democratic Party from 2005 through 2012. Also in retirement, she chose to write poetry instead of continuing her academic career, having found an extraordinary community of poets in Door County, Wisconsin. The two strands, poetry and politics, kept coming together in poems for critique in writing groups from 2006 to the present, and connections were enriched both by sailing to Ontario, Canada a dozen times and traveling with Overseas Adventure Travel to countries she never expected to visit. From 2006 to 2018, she published four chapbooks with Finishing Line Press. This is her first full-length book of poems, although she has authored or co-authored three academic books.

As Poet Laureate of Door County in 2013-2015, she founded the Door County Poets Collective to edit *Soundings: Door County in Poetry* (Caravaggio Press, 2015) and *Halfway to the North Pole: Door County in Poetry* (Four Windows Press, 2020). She and Francha Barnard co-edited the *2017 Wisconsin Poets Calendar* for Wisconsin Fellowship of Poets.

She continues to call Door County home, but since 2021, when their son died suddenly of a pulmonary embolism, she and her husband have spent winters in Ames, Iowa to be with their grandsons and daughter-in-law. She also takes every opportunity to visit her daughter, son-in-law, and granddaughters in Chicago, San Diego and the San Juan Islands. She and her husband are grateful to have lived at a time in the US when two kids from farm families could attend a fine university and become members of a strong middle class with access to the arts, great libraries and continuing education. The US has been a wonderful place to live, and we hope to extend the advantages we have experienced to all others who make it their home.

www.ingramcontent.com/pod-product-compliance
Lightning Source LLC
Chambersburg PA
CBHW050447150626
46551CB00029B/1985